ELLIPSES

Poorva Trikha

Leadstart
INKSTATE

ISBN 978-93-5667-042-6

First published in India 2022 by Leadstart Inkstate
A brand of One Point Six Technologies Pvt. Ltd.

Office No. 116, Building No. A-3,
B Wing, BGTA Ganga CHS,
Wadala Truck Terminal Road, Mumbai – 400037.
Phone: +91 96999 33000
Email: info@leadstartcorp.com
www.leadstartcorp.com

Disclaimer: The views expressed in this book are those of the Author and do not pertain to be held by the Publisher.

Editor: Shayoni Mitra
Cover: R. Maharaja
Layouts: Sathish Kumar

Dedicated to:

The Anonymous Reader

About the Book

The proposed book titled "Ellipsis" contains poems that are reflective, romantic and spiritual in nature. Some of these poems express the yearnings of the poet for her unfulfilled dreams, some pertain to her experiences of motherhood and some of them are Worthworthian in essence and exhibit her poetic interactions with Nature. The poems are worded in simple language and cover a wide variety of the poetess' experiences as a woman, as a wife, as a teacher and as a mother to a toddler. It took the author 8 years to complete the manuscript because of her personal engagements and professional responsibilities. But despite being immersed in the worldly life, she grabbed the opportunities that came to her just as the light enters a room through a little slit in the curtain, to write these verses. The title itself suggests that the book contains poems that were written between the spaces, or conveys the idea of things that the poetess could not have expressed out loud. The deliberately left out words, found a home in the poems contained in this manuscript.

About the Author

Poorva Trikha has been working as an Assistant Professor in English at GGDSD college, Chandigarh since 2014. She has been writing poetry since the age of 12 and has previously published two books titled "Leftover Ink" and "Photojournalism". She did her PhD in English from the Department of English and Cultural Studies at Panjab University. Academically driven, she won a Gold Medal from Panjab University for her MPhil in the year 2013. This is her second book of poems comprising verses that she has written over a span of eight years. These poems encompass her experiences as a professor, as a wife, as a mother and as someone who ponders over life's circumstances in tranquility. She has published many research papers in reputable National and International Journals. Her poems have been published in many periodicals including *The Tribune*, *The Criterion* and *Muse India*. Her deepest interests include reading, writing, cooking and crocheting. She writes routinely at her Instagram page @wordedvoid.

Acknowledgements

I would like to thank the entire team of Leadstart for making this book a reality and for bringing it to life in the exact way I envisioned. I owe my sincerest gratitude to the talented artist – Benita, who very generously supplied the cover for the book.

Contents

–01–

Ellipses

From one mirror to another,
I look for myself,
under the dome of names
and social media tags,
I get effaced.

From pole to pole,
I search for a cover,
avoiding sirens
and looking for corners,
I tend to disappear.

From a call to another,
typed words in a chat box,
my eyes search for meaning,
the sense of which,
escapes me.

Where am I?
I ask the ground.
Who am I?
I ask the sky
that flees me.

Maybe this is what I Am…
a question mark,
an exclamation,
or just a comma, that
eludes these ellipses.

–02–

Outside Plato's Cave

What could it have been?
To think of have bartered
the arête of the mind
for a bunch of smiles
and nights unknown…
for those initial pleasantries
and eternal woes,
for the evenings of Poker
and Dice filled noons
…to think of having traded wisely,
but later recounting the loss!

Who could it have been?
A knight of labour who
burns the midnight oil
to attain that cloud,
or that modern artist
who instead of a brush

picked a dark void
to enclose eternity
into an image?
...to think of having chosen with forethought
that only lead to a slumber!

How could it have been?
To imagine new lands
with faces, read only in books,
tombstones, epitaphs and Arthur's seat?
To walking on pebbled roads
of grey or white
all sold or given up
for a full lap
and some hard earned coos,
for toothless joy
and sleepless pleasures
...to feel having acted instinctively
but having ended up in the wrong lane!

When could it have been?
The coffee houses filled with smoke
or bald heads and big glasses
or holograms and phone blocs
with airel humankind?
To have seized the day
for those popcorns and reels
and for loudly playing countdown

for overtly religious eves
and social atheism
…to believe that time was right,
but to have held on too long!

It is what else could never have been…
a mosaic of zig-zag thoughts
reclining on a c-shaped pillow
or a rotating high chair
the sense of a beating heart
that takes a beating
for its little satisfactions and
ever fleecing perfection…

–03–

Love Wins, Always

There's a slot in a jigsaw,
that only you can fit into.
There's a grand scheme of things,
waiting for your arrival…
Arrive, as you are,
bring your hurt,
stapled around your being,
hugging you, and thereby,
protecting you from falling apart.

Shakyamuni found a way of life,
that millions of Buddhists follow,
so did Nanak, so did Rama,
the way of Kosen-rufu,
the way for our humane lives, lived fully,
traversing only through love.

And love doesn't have an address;
it doesn't live at a place, or in a person,
or in an idea or a moment.
It's what we're made of,
beyond rejection,
and our little heartbreaks.
So come as you are!
lovingly and loved in turn,
because
in the end,
love wins,
always Always ALWAYS.

–04–

En Attendant

Some random thoughts in my heart
Decided to revolt
Against the conventions, the set rules,
Miss Arbitrary led the march
With Mr Anarchy in the vanguard
Temples, Religions, Customs,
All human made things sank,
Into the novel ray of the new horizon

The price of excellence
Is routine dedication
To undying devotion
To a dying cause.
It's neither the fruit
Nor the root,
But the compulsion to become,
Something more than itself,
A transformation, an imago, a zenith.

You may leave a small town,
But the small town never leaves you.
It's in the very nature of attention,
To the petty, the human, the mundane,
The lack of indifference,
the idleness of the scheming mind,
And the loyalty to the norm,
It's difficult for the Future to fathom,
The difference between the smallness of big towns,
And the bigness of the small ones.

April came again but with Auden this time,
Through the roads laden with hopes,
Of meeting a joyous face,
And enlivening a classroom.
The wallet musters force,
to dwell carefree in the grand malls and local bazaars.
Fuel, Recharge and Bank balance,
Brewed in a whistleless pot, to pour a happy life.

Her face shines like diamonds,
Laid on a beautiful beach with the cleanest sands,
All fish, shells, and foot stamps withdrew,
To let her tiny feet stand,
Unsteadily, untidily,
In a beauty that revokes,
The right of man to gaze,
Such unquestionable, unintelligible,
Glaze.

The closures await,
Apprehensive and in anticipation,
Of a day that never arrives,
Despite the spinning longitudes and
Receding nights.
Peace is asocial by nature,
And so is happiness.
They meet at the same spot,
Where Isolation plays with Art.
The moment to let go, the painless goodbye,
Never comes.

Numbers and the Alphabet,
Are a part of the circus,
Which runs from start to end,
With unanswered questions and
Thousands of distractions,
From Womb to Grave,
Entertained all the way,
With Food, Books, Love and Toys,
The focus from the real is,
Perpetually procrastinated.

What must be asked?
Who must be obeyed?
Where must one look?
The infinity mark stares,
Back like a boomerang,

Which a peddler catches,
Puts into his pocket,
And quietly goes back to munch,
The peanuts in his hand.

–05–

Gates & Jobs

The lion knows the whereabouts of the rabbit,
But the rabbit thinks he is outsmarting the lion by hiding,
He celebrates his freedom, his sense, his art,
While the lion awaits the right time as a tactical gambit.

So one day it finally came, the moment to confront,
Roared the lion, and tried to startle the rabbit from behind,
The rabbit looked back at him with rage and parity in his eyes,
Such that the lion was taken aback by an affront.

"Did you think I was trying to hide?" questioned the white being,
With clenching paws and grinding teeth, the lion made reply,
"You'll be dead before you know it," and breathed an angry sigh,
The rabbit gently put on his face a smile while disagreeing.

Such Conviction, Such Stability, Such Prick – the lion did impress,

With less thought and more awe, the rabbit he did enroll,

As his personal guard, his wingman and thought of eating him no more,

With strength of mind and faith, the rabbit achieved his success.

Months went by and all was in mirth,

They moved about in the jungle with insouciance,

When boredom stuck, or walks went lonely,

The rabbit's playfulness and wit proved its worth.

Neither real ferociousness nor savagery; in every way unfit,

A canny but tender rabbit bewitchingly survived,

A giant force of nature and a quickly served death,

Through a path that only Courage could see, instinct would remiss.

Forever now and before, whenever Valour has tried,

With acuity and an unfailing belief of accomplishment,

The globe has bent, the sky has risen, storms have gone quiet,

To let the new paths form, to let novel voices preside.

–06–

To Pain

Once upon a time,

Pain knocked at Love's door.

But she didn't answer.

Then it crept in through the windows,

She blocked it with ironic bars of her imagination.

Then it tried to climb in through the chimneys of
misunderstandings,

But she smoked it out with poetry.

Then one fine day,

Tired of fighting the inevitable,

She decided to courageously brave the winds of loneliness,

Stormed out of her home and let Pain,

Along with its entire army of gloom,

Rain all over her,

around her, about her,

drench her very being.

When the sun rose again,
she looked within to find,
that she was still soaking
with her-amorous self,
Love's sunshine shone,
reminding her of Gibran's,
"Your pain is the breaking
of the shell that encloses
your understanding"
And understanding,
in all its forms
celebrates
love!

–07–

In Gaia's Garden

Over a cup of tea,
We shared,
An evaporating moment of beauty.

Outside On the patio laze three quiet hounds,
Algae laden pond with fish abounds,
Deep coloured wilderness-lush and green,
Wind Chimes on trees enlivening the scene,
No familiar voice or language humane,
Reserves of silence and peace regained,

Sitting inside that cottage – just you and me,
In that instant – a flash of eternity,
Your deep eyes filled with amour,
Those dewy lips – soft and demure,
My beats paced when you threw a glance,
Realities melted in that instance.

Over a cup of tea,
We shared,
An evaporating moment of beauty.

–08–

The Ascent

I shall not stop,
At your calls for duty,
For I hear an inner voice,
Commanding a selfish beauty.

My dreams are glued to the wings,
Of labour and self service of my goals,
No matter how you claim or chain me,
They'll easily slip through the falls.

Would I be fair to you with an unfulfilled heart?
With preposterous smiles and vacant identity?
Neither is this a stage nor will I wear the mask,
So let's face the truth with objective simplicity.

My path does lay before me,
Inviting, Exciting, Calling,
Let my steps proceed freely,
Ere the drums of revolt starts rolling!

–09–

On Getting Married

Prosaic words sing,
Something out of nothing,
Fallen leaves entwine,
Sunlit paths rhyme,
Clouds on sky's bosom dance,
Birds float under a trance,
Fountains of amorous springs,
Hark now! The church bell rings.

Winds in hair cuddle and play,
Random hearts leap and sway,
The cliff's zenith, Sisyphus receives,
An expecting mother crochets and weaves.
The typing stano tunes a composer,
A ballerino on toes woos her!
Under the bower the two of us sit,
Flicker on like lamps dim lit.

Pours down your disarming charm,

To complete the moon curve on my palm;

Our italicised lives call for celebration!

–10–

Into the Void

You're so far–
Like a starry night overlooking my window.
The world of distance between us,
And the world of difference between our thoughts,
This Grim gift of loneliness,
Rises from the longing in the heart,
Puffs and dies on the window panes.
Grills of patience and,
The hope of fruit laden tree outside,
Entertain my emotional stances.
These stretched glances,
Finding no converging image inside the eyes,
Return empty handed and blur the,
Time lost.

O it's true that it's all over.
Gone by. Beatless and Breathless in moments. Then,
Let's not be gods and go beyond the unsaid.
This window and the star lit darkness,
Are both just a dream.

–11–

The Flow

These ever in transition,
Thoughts and emotions,
Bind us, grind us, sometimes blind us.
Dragging life down to others' smiles,
Others' nods, their cries,
and their locked brows.

Sitting gloomily at night looking out of the window,
Or joyfully chattering on a chair in the lawn,
We are driven through and through,
And bound slavishly in chains of servitude,
Imposed by the chemical lords of our bodies.

That old memory brought some tears the other day,
And that new laurel did fill the heart with pride,
This way or that, emotions somersault on our nerves,
Treating us, the poor, as an ever changing archive.

But what is life then?

If the hurt doesn't sting or if love doesn't arouse Ecstasy?

A mute tree that can't dance unless the winds blow or the roots uproot.

This self-hegemonic state of our lives,

Such a creative recipe for commemoration!

So grand! So glorious! So Naïve!

O then! Embrace gently, each moment,

For what it's worth, Change is the only permanence!

–12–

Be You

It burns them high and low,
To watch the other one go,
And get better,
And get bigger,
And get higher,
It breeds jealousies for awakening
Their inadequacies.
Beats them wet and dry,
To behold the other shine,
And do greater,
And become larger,
And reach wider,
It incepts envy for laying bare,
Their inabilities.
Hurts them about and around,
To see the other amaze,
And succeed further,
And conquer more,

And progress farther,
It gathers malice for exposing to them,
Their weaknesses.
Pains then above and below,
To witness the other grow,
And love harder,
And stay longer,
And dive deeper,
It garners avarice for uncovering
Their cowardice.

But life's not about them,
So their snares, outlive and outdo,
Your beautiful life is ultimately,
And Audaciously, All about you.

–13–

At Last

It's always the storms raging inside,
That turn mild waves into wild tides,
As you look through the binoculars, you'll see,
How her mooning self today, is running free.

A Silent shore with starfish and shells,
Castles in Heavens with chiming bells,
Garlands, wreaths and laurels on margins,
Are all that she is able to imagine.

The ship will sink and the boat will rise,
There will be no mermaids, no lies,
Look through the chaos directly,
You'll see,
The Truth will proudly claim its victory.

–14–

One For Two

I was taught that I want to do this,
that my inner longings will outrun me,
if I don't.

He will be kind, I learnt to believe,
generous and polite,
to the possible extent.
Beyond which,
I was on my own.

The truths that I was told,
caught up with me,
no sooner than,
I began reading again.

The fights I lost and the
poems I never wrote,
couldn't slumber further.

I memorized it all,
the latent affronts,
the superficial compliments,
all of which, I learnt, make
a perfectly happy life.

But someone forgot to lock my words,
or yours or many others'
and so we write, the story of who we are,
or would have been or shall be!

–15–

Rehab For Love

There should be a Rehab for love,
Those sleepless nights of passion,
And the delicate pain of yearning,
All those flashbacks and,
never ending burning,
We need a rehab for love.

Lovers should have access to Lethe,
Those mental imprints,
and the melodies we chased,
All those special touches,
and chiming aftertaste,
We need to wash it all down away.

Lovers need a new world,
where parting never happens,
and palms don't sweat,
Where money and matter don't matter,

and families are not a threat,
We need a braver newer world.

Lovers should be allowed in Heaven,
after all the beauty they added,
and the floral fragrant lives they lived,
After eternally poetic verses they wrote,
and the unloving world they survived.
We need a new heaven for lovers.

–16–

Hope

She stood in the balcony,
waiting to see him,
but he refused to show up,
the son, the spouse, the father.

On the frontlines of medicine,
or in the lines of the Police,
or the man behind the supply chain,
he was braving it all.

He stood watching the gate,
eagerly with anticipatory eyes,
but she wasn't anywhere nearby,
the mother, the wife, the daughter.

Counselling or Nursing a patient
or planning the course of action
or gearing up for the prime time report
she was fearless in the face of harsh winds.

———

While this one just sat and crocheted,
that one was too happy to be on the couch
glued to netflix, hotstar or prime,
(For when does 'chill' justify being
a euphemism for indolence)?

Then there is her,
who organised her whole bookshelf
and read the unread books,
and then there is him,
who finally learnt to make tea,
and grew his first plant,
right from its seed.

————

The elderly say,
they have never seen "Such Times"
The politicians declare,
that they have never done "Such Service"
The economists profess,

"There'll be unfathomable economic destruction"
The newspapers read,
"The virus is wreaking havoc"
and – Little children,
well, they are just happy
to have their parents home.

One mourns for the people who lost their lives,
and fills with rage for the unchecked spread
if/which/(do we know for sure?) could have been
prevented.

Is cleaner air, compensation enough?

How long, before we go back to old ways?
Drive without a reason,
and write without a rhyme,
and live life recklessly again.

The planet shall keep spinning,
so will the sunshine,
What can then change?
This/That/ Him/ Her/ Them–
or Us!

In the end,
when nothing remains,
there's Hope.

There's hope for change.
There's hope for rebirth.
There's hope for 'Word'.

Here's hoping,
this is a start.

–17–

Spaces Of Erasure

Dear Plath,
I write to you again.
I met some of our other friends-
Amrita, Mary and Nelly
out in the open day.
We talked of love,
and how it is selfish,
and how the louts will never understand.
Out in the open day,
without the walls, you know!

You once wrote,
"I hurl my heart, to halt your pace"
but things have now changed
and we prefer to keep our hearts
right where they belong.

We left it all,
for the sake of our souls,
and yet,
no Gods came forward,
nothing happened,
Neither rain nor thunder.

Anna once mentioned,
"There are many kinds of love
as there are hearts"
but back then we didn't know,
besides, it is true,
our passions exceeded
the invisible hedges.

We are the outcasts,
and nothing'd just fit
how could we relent?
So we played to the tunes
of our handpans,
wildly,
and here we are,
all lonely again!

So I write to you once more
for when can unrequited silence
ever remain unheard?

–18–

Blossoms

I will watch the sunsets,
And hear the chorus of the skies,
just once when kitchen work ends,
and baby learns to walk.

The beauty of being with the self,
and indulging in personal wealth,
is knocking at the distant door...
Floating poets are waiting to be ashore.

A million pearls thrown,
somewhere in mind strewn,
eager for the baby baths to end,
and midnight feedings to dispend.

Words on pages waiting for a pair of eyes,
the lone pen in a folded journal lies,
hoping that the bibs will dry soon,
and sudden tantrums won't fill the room.

They are anticipating me,
my nursery of thoughts and philosophy,
where one day the chores will disappear,
and the beauty of motherhood will persevere.

Those stuttering initial words,
are the sweetest sounds that ever occurred,
this constant demand for attention,
certainly makes me feel special.

Her imaginary world where animals lounge,
the dolls speak and innocence abounds,
is a state of joy and pleasure to see,
blissful are these times – for her & me!

Oh let them bide quite,
for I am living the poetry I write
My muse isn't pausing for slumber,
Just that these moments, muses outnumber.

They are shaping the field,
and planting the seeds,
that someday into verses will blossom,
reserving me a name in ambrosil macrocosm.

–19–

I Write of You

Between the imagined spaces of my poetry,

I write you.

Sometimes casually, sometimes with caution,

You are the secret I hide,

Under the folds of my saree,

Or inside the hem of my pillow,

Inside the pen between my fingers,

And under the social smile.

At times breathing out to the night sky,

The moon hears your name,

Or the rustling of dry leaves,

Spell it out to my company,

But I hush it,

Closely behind the curtain of conversation,

Slipping it gently to the back of my mind,

To unwrap,

When the voices are gone,

And lull plays its melody,

Of a deep-rooted romance,
Into the hungry ears of sleeping flowers,
I write of you.
Occasionally on paper,
Mostly on thoughts,
To be blown away,
Just so that the new day,
Bring in the blossoms,
Of your mauve memories,
That beautify my world on the inside,
And remain an untold tale,
A myth in making,
A poignant reality that fiction,
Shies away from.
You are mine to keep,
Within me, exuberantly,
Ever fertile, ever mellow,
Euphoniously ascending,
As a scent that lingers,
In the glimmer of my eyes,
And the words of my prosaic life,
Invisibly disguised as the colour on my lips,
The flair in my gait,
The life in my body,
The poem residing on the tip of my fingers,
I write of you.

–20–

Our Lemon Tree

The tree that looks bare
but hides a hundred lemons
in fact bears about fifty
yellow green lime spheres
reminds me
of a time when rains
would supress the thunder
blocking the way
just so it could pour
silently,
without much show
of awe, of surprise or alert.
Tiny spheres decorating
piggy pig tongues
of little children in
unicorn wellies
being shouted to
for not keeping their umbrellas straight.

Just a few drops
and the cheese splits,
noses curl
eyes get shut
and soda pops.
Home grown,
with fresh smelling leaves
next to a tall papaya tree,
that lusciously stands,
the humble lemon tree awaits,
the sounds of little children
jumping in puddles
and hoping for the clouds to
never part.

–21–

Beeji

Oral folklore,
Ballads learnt in adolescence,
Scores of wedding ditties,
Funeral songs memorized.

Evolving garments,
Frocks worn on swings,
That bridal Lehnga,
And a lifetime of suits

Thoughtless Food,
Candies of tamarind,
Millions of chapattis rolled,
And semi liquid diet for toothless jaws.

Multiple existences,
A playful girl,
A dutiful wife,
A thoughtful mother evermore.

–22–

Definitions

Someone wanted a name,
a Dr., perhaps or Adv. or Er.
While everyone became someone,
Someone remained noone.

Everyone told her it mattered
Being someone,
Who is someone,
Everyone looks up to.

Noone mentioned,
That Someone could be,
Whoever she wanted to be,
Without asking/telling anybody.

Someone really wanted to be noone
she thought it befitting,
to unhear whatever says everyone,
and to follow her intent.

While everyone became someone,
Someone became noone,
Everyone now has a name,
And she has what noone has.

She, who I talk of,
is happy, much
like Emily,
who became someone,
by being nobody.

–23–

Cannot, Shall Not, Won't

There is a voice that I have,
that wasn't endowed to me at birth.
It came to me gradually,
like wings,
and grew word by word,
as I spread my verses.
This is the voice of my fight,
it is what carries my truth,
bare, sweet, honest, galling.

For better or for worse,
this voice found me,
under the bed on a dark night,
under the stars at dawn,
or under the burden,
of those hundreds of thousands,
secrets that I was told to hush about.

'Lean back on yourself
lean in to thyself
lean on to that voice
that rustles between your hmm's
that tussle with the boundaries and
that refuses to be quiet.'

This is my preface.
This too, could be, an epilogue to my life.

"I can not,
Shall not,
Won't,
Shut up!"

–24–

A Revelation

Mr Toby had no life, or some would say,

But he did have a pretty wife, who never said nay.

To gain glory, garlands and greatness,

He worked night and day.

Idle pleasures, time with children,

Dinners & Romances: were all tossed away.

Thus, the graph of progress was kept on a rise,

Awards, Honours, Laurels, were then not a surprise.

One fine day, sitting silently in his lawn, Mr Toby did realise,

What if the whole purpose of living is 'otherwise'?

What if prestige is an illusion and fame, just a scam,

What if absorbing life with its wonders is original grand plan?

That single time walk, that special last kiss,
What if behind these tiny moments hides bliss?
All the ceaseless toil and relentless chase,
What if these don't ensure him that eternal place?

Mr Toby got up from his chair and breathed in new,
His head was up and his warm lips, a smile did pursue.
Luther or Newton or Gandhi or Christ,
Their posthumous renown came in lieu of their presents' scarifce.

He hummed a ditty and swung his arms,
Every view in sight set forth its innate charm,
Never did a blossom or a birthday Mr Toby missed,
His heart and mind thus kept their newly found tryst.

–25–

Rings

There is no love here.
He goes in and washes out,
seldom, to fulfil,
some random fantasy,
or an office.

There is love,
abundant, overflowing,
right behind the clock,
weaving in some memory threads,
and positioned,
right before the world pushed in.

Beautiful!
Oh, it's beautiful.
his hands, those veins,
his scented arms,
every little word,
all flowers twained.

There is music somewhere,
silently playing on the chords of my heart,
or perhaps his too.
I hear the beats clasping,
the clappings of thoughts,
of a distant reunion.

Hold my hand,
and hold my hand,
both are my walking companions,
forever preventing, a mis-step,
a fall, and rousing in the air,
a mix of suave lavender &
a thorny, wild rose.

–26–

Balsam

… balsam…
the greatest incomplete melody
whose composer
lost his fingers
over a very trivial
break of heart…

Why did he forget
that pain is a privilege
leading to conception
of deeper hearts' beating
plus
nothing really ever dies!

The bud that falls
with or without autumn
blends with the soil
and enriches the sense

with its crushed
repertoire.

He was gone
not without an invite
to liberate the times
smothering under
the garb of tradition
and decedent/vintage carriage.

Does time really move?
or do we look up to a machine?
A cake baked by self
to celebrate one's birthday
on the occasion
that deserves no speciality.

Anyway,
let's just close the books now
too much with wisdom already
the dying sun awaits
for an evening Azan
and the innocence
of an unlettered bosom.

–27–

Beyond Time and Space

Above the daily,
high on a spiritual pedestal,
lives the feeling,
that refuses to die down.

Beyond the chores,
near the horizon,
lives the feeling,
that refuses to fade out.

Engaged beside the mind,
butterflies contained,
it flourishes,
on the island of hope.

To give and to not expect,
a gift of worth,
of a lifetime of fire,
it glimmers and gleams.

Dreams of unity,
of a raga unsung,
plays in the background,
to the melody of faith.

You and I,
with or without,
never apart,
dissolving divinely!

–28–

March On

For what you call life today,
Will be another tale some day,
Thrown together like pawns on a chart,
It twists or rises or tumbles away.

Without an orientation or instruction guide,
Tread your own path in your gait,
None to follow but many fingers to hold,
It wades away without the wait.

The tower that once was an underground arch,
Now aims to kiss the sky,
With nothing but ladders of the mind,
Tiptoeing with a willful drive or a low sigh.

When the devil created the days,
God carefully designed the nights,
To breathe in rest and contemplate,
The ideas that timelessly shine bright.

–29–

A Kid at the Lights

I'm a Bartender!
Tendering to the bars,
of your discrimination.
I am an atheist,
professing allegiance to multiple religions.
I hold no God in my eyes,
nor powers in these beads.
These buttons on my young shoulders,
tie me to some inherent devilry.
My un-surmountable spirit,
is a greater evolution,
than your well-bred civility,
will ever comprehend.
You see me at the lights
and you scowl,
You see me in the park,
and you grimace,
and here I am,

Nevertheless,
with a spider silk backbone,
Standing!
I need no education,
that your schools can give,
Nor no skills,
that your schemes offer,
My survival is my reward,
and my silence is my gift to you.

–30–

A Sonnet on the Ad Page

Size 0,

Fair & Bright,

Begetting at least twenty lakhs,

Obedient, respectful,

Not to forget –

Suitable to the Boy's height,

A good cook,

Low maintenance, High Class,

Well-read: Unapplied,

Well bread: Unexposed,

Well Spoken: Unexercised,

No other attached strings,

All we need for our ordinary son,

Are just these basic things.

–31–

A Rhapsody

Dear Poetry,
Why wouldn't you leave me?
Under the clouds of words,
Why'd you come to me?
Like a lovable shih-tzu,
Beckoning me near,
You make me indulge me.

Pulling my thoughts one by one,
And kneading them into expressions,
Sometimes like wet rain drops,
Falling from the leaves of my sapodilla tree,
You gently slide through my mind,
Until conjuringly, wirelessly,
I jot you down on paper to free.

The world tries constantly,
To overthrow my rhyme,

Amidst the hustle and bustle that pursues,
For relief, I turn to you.
You pull me through the synapse,
And bring me to the abbey
For a tranquil rendezvous.

You grab me through my senses,
And arouse me with passion,
With the enigma that you are.
Like a storm at times,
the let gones find their voice,
much like a calm sea sometimes,
you cancel the tidal noise.

As a mother sometimes does,
you unexpectedly disappoint,
much like a daughter sometimes,
all unfulfilled dreams you anoint.
You are the lover who never parts,
You are my Lolita, You are Binodini,
In you, lies the key to eternity.

Dear Poetry,
You and I together-
We're a beautiful rhapsody.

–32–

Nix

No!
That was the thing they heard,
When she spoke her first word,
That was the only time she could,
Honestly and truthfully express,
Coiled in innocence and pure,
Thoughts: her stance.

No!
How was that ever acceptable again?
Neither to the father nor to the husband,
Neither to the boss nor to the maid,
Neither to the mind nor to the heart.

No!
How that rings! Echoes from
Millions of painful crevices around the world.
No! That vibration!

That hidden treble.
That thud!
This two-letter word,
in one syllable,
binds within
the tragic truth of all compliance.

–33–

On a Visit to the Zoo

Very close to my house,
lives a white tiger,
two timid lions and a couple of jaguars,
hopping around in the Sun,
some wild cats, some pea fowls,
and lazily lounging Hippopotamus,
two enwinged by their tails, crocodiles
and a pair of pythons.

I took my year old, little daughter,
to meet them "as they are",
with anticipatory joy,
at her wonder-filled amazement.
They were there, out in the sun,
with no shade to rest in or hide,
Hunters forbidden to hunt, birds prohibited to fly,
they sleep when human noises dull,
eat whatever they are fed with, whenever.
thrill-less, naked, expressionless!

As I lull my baby to sleep,
inside the cosy comfort of her home,
a part of me shudders at the thought,
of what it would feel like,
if leopards, emus and elephants,
came to sight see me or her 'us',
The after thoughts rush me:
that sight of perhaps a mama bear,
encaged in what 'maybe' looks like wilderness,
all those vacant eyes, that lifelessness,
that merely sustains them,
but devours "who they are".

I wonder if I'd ever go again.

–34–

It's Okay to Not be Okay

It's okay to not be okay.
Out in the cold nights,
when the moon tries to hide,
the stars all wait for your face,
but it's okay to not show up!

All our broken stars like hearts,
trying to gather their shine,
waddling through the jungles,
of unfulfilled desires,
which eyes undermine,
It's okay to not be okay.

If I try to hold your hand,
and your hand feels dank,
if I try to touch your neck,
and your breath feels damp,
it's okay to slowly push back,
and quietly walk away.

If love is true, O! if it is true,
your steps will retreat,
and you'll sit beside me,
under the sacred tree,
and with your eyes mild and soft,
unfurl the secrets of my soul.

Till then, it's okay to take time,
to make room or find a rhyme,
step back and muster courage,
to again be organically mine.

It's okay to not be okay for now,
and it's okay to take time.

–35–

Educated Housewives

It rhymed,
it rhymed,
it rhymed,
until it stopped.

The waves kissed each other,
and the sun hugged itself,
the clouds held hands,
and rivers flew in unison.

Lines emerged following one another,
couplets, belonging together,
some anecdotal fragrances,
of stories told in symbols.

It raged – the storm,
and Apollo did not relent,
rains debarred the clouds,
confluence dried up.

No similies and no commas,
the sonnet emerged blank,
from raisin hearts and,
rusted minds.

The best of them,
done with themselves,
dusted into households,
framing their theses into hidden drawers.

–36–

On an Evening Stroll

On my evening stroll to the park today,
four poems wrote themselves through me.

In March, my city blooms Petunias,
numerous, voilet and red and pink,
and the ones with stripes,
colourful tigers' like,
bravely standing through the
initial summer heat.

The not too rich Bougainvilleas,
Fill the outer boundaries of homes,
Daisies in parks and marigolds,
and periwinkles thrive in pots,
inside the mini lawns…
in all of this,
a scrap dealer
scavenges for useful broken twigs,

or leftover beer bottles,
on this rugged bicycle with ragged sacks,
that almost forgot,
they were once white,
in the corners of a posh, gated society.

Few little children,
coaxing their mothers to pluck,
unripe mulberries,
unwary of the stains,
wait in a hoard,
while a poor woman's daughter,
goes up reverse on a giant metallic slide,
unwatched but self conscious
completely unbothered by a unknown enemy
that rages and unnerves the world.

My little missy,
decides to sit sideways on her,
tricycle pushed through the back handle,
and doesn't care for the free peddle,
that revolves in wilderness.
She likes the swing of her shadow,
and insists that her hair remain untied,
She goes till Wednesday in a tune,
and then happily and suddenly,
Saturday arrives.

Our dear poets saw these,
and pondered about life and its agony,
a nightingale inspired the unspeakable once,
daffodils once created history,
Alice was perhaps born on one such evening.
All the beauty of this conspired,
to meet these minds and surprise their eyes,
at said given moment in time,
today it came and touched me,
the Glory of creation in its sovereignity.

But O! the misery of the unseeing eye,
and the ignorance of familiarity.

–37–

Allons Donc

Woe are the lovers, Who live under the same roof,
There's a world of beauty that from them itself removes.

Love needs distance for itself to breathe free,
It takes a faraway 'you' to contain a close 'me'.

How do the pedestrian lovers, standing hand in hand commune,
The couplets of passion or make sense of the exotic moon?

The void in their hearts their movie dates can perhaps never fill,
We immersed ourselves in each other's void, for amour, to distil.

Their reality is in fact too dull for a story,
And our hyper-real world is worthy of eternal glory.

When can words ever be enough? Or a kiss Or a caress?
It indeed takes a god to make intangible love to a goddess.

Allons donc! We shall never the norm to ourselves compare,
For when can others comprehend our exultation extraordinaire?

–38–

Vermilion Florets

Things they are a changin',
a Rosa Juliet that in solitude bloomed,
In the midst of lonely woods,
has been visited by the drops of rain,
gentle, fondling,
caresses of yens,
seeing which,
a hermit peacock has decided to dance,
with its exuberant feathers.

Colours have evolved,
azure, teal, iris,
the sky has decided to tilt its head,
as it kisses the earthly lips,
with its moonlit tongue.

Behold the words running,
sliding through the air into sublime,

leaving behind the two vermilion florets,
to swing through sunlit vistas,
into timeless horizons
and build a cottage there…
where…autumn never arrives,
the sun is docilely warm,
and the moon is always beheld.

–39–

Aloha Brahma!

Little did the seed know,
It carries a world inside.
The rain that fell,
Hardly knew it's supporting a life.
The oblivious soil,
Never dreamt that it's worthy
Of laying claim,
To what language calls "Beauty"

Beauty ~
That in ignorance sprouts,
Mute to the onlookers' comments,
Unconscious of the eyes,
Drawing on its own belief
of finding its purpose:

'to live itself is the meaning'

Aloha Brahma!
Hail Gaia!

–40–

Ivy

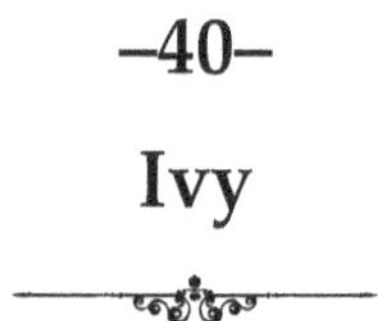

I kept my love a secret,
Drawing 'in' my breaths more,
It hid beneath my heart,
Very close to the soul.

Appearing bare and colourless outside,
Love kept creeping deeper inside,
It lay inside my gut,
Rose up and fell in mind,
Sometimes softened my knees,
Many a time my hand declined.
Concealed from the general view,
It found its internal routes,
Running through my veins,
Looking through my eyes,
It tingled my toes,
And it caressed my thighs.

"Oh that boy's just plain.

Maybe a little indifferent too", they said,

Good Shiva! When could they see,

The mosaic that his simpleness let be,

It wasn't long before it overtook,

The emptiness of my nights,

And made me draw out,

A long sigh,

Of spring,

Of love,

Of him,

Growing through me.

–41–

Conversation with the Mirror

I love you.

Let me hold your hand.

Cry if you will.

Look up, look at me.

It's okay.

We're friends.

We can touch.

Come with me.

Let me show you a box.

Each of these bottles is a memory.

Remember that Lake!

You looked like a dandy.

Why is it a big deal?

Let me kiss you to tell,

it's all good.

We're all by ourselves.

Do you need a hug?
Here.
Rightly.

Now look up.
We can star gaze.
You can caress my tresses.
I would only smile.
Can I lean on you?
It's so warm here.
I am happy.
You're H-A-P-P-Y,
Aren't we?

–42–

Poetry of the Prosaic

The world only remembers the extraordinary.
For the ordinary are remembered
in the hearts of those
who they loved.

The extraordinary in science
became Nobels, Newtons and Einsteins,
The overzealous in love,
are hailed as Cleopatras, Ranjhas and Helens,
The exceptional at sports,
count themselves as Alis, Bolts and Philips.

This doctor who earnestly cured every sore,
and the nurse who took care of a delusional man,
the teacher who sponsored the education of many,
and the cook who served the queen honorarily,
will all be forgotten someday.

The poetry of the prosaic,
the music of the silent,
the beauty of the unseen,
and the art of the artless,
thrive in secret places.
Behind the curtains of theatres,
under the starlit places,
right in the centre of the forest,
or in the middle of commotion,
the most extraordinary,
 roam anonymously,
content with the prize,
of having breathed,
especially.

–43–

To Battered Heart

Dear Battered Heart,
Look at that plucked petunia,
or that fallen periwinkle,
it's short lives been torn away,
at the whim of a lover.

See that little boy there?
Yonder, under that lonely tree?
He just lost his father
and isn't bothered about the pain,
but is thinking about how to make a living.

That sheep over the barn,
no one took its permission,
before stripping away,
all of its wintery dome.
See how it cannot complain

The cows that bear their udders hurting,
the eyes that view devilry under the table,
all those sailors who didn't see the morn light,
and all those children who were forcefully wed,
our Sun is a witness to them all.

Your little ache,
is just another heartbreak,
that pinches like a fork,
stabbed at the back of the neck,
but by troth is, seulement,
an alighting from the bubble amour.

Pick up these sore pieces,
and paint them white,
Softly wipe off the tears,
and walk upright,
for a well mended wall,
is sometimes stronger,
than a poorly kept fort.

–44–

Time

I would like to wear time,
on my frail wrist and,
calculate the length of each hour,
with fond memories.

For what else does one have?
On this unexplained journey,
where,
the worst of moments,
get easily forgotten, and
the best of memories,
are eventually overwrit.

The happiest of times,
becomes just another story.
The most tragic days,
for "Time heals everything", they say,
become a casual passé!

So let me absorb,

this 'now-ness'

this daylily,

of genuine smiles,

and leave the past for learning,

and rest the future for poetry.

–45–

Summers

Being a full adult
has revealed to me
things that I never knew
measures that didn't exist
parameters that were unthought of.

To begin earning at the right age
And to settle down with a decent boy
And to listen to the biological clock
To Touch the feet and wash the linen
And to definitely smile at guests.

Sitting in a hostel balcony
I used to look at my watch
to take cognizance of time
(of when the meals will be served again
The most fresh chapatis
and hot dal that soon would

end up looking like a clump of sand.)
It's now the yawning of my girl
or the redness on her eyelids
that tell me that the night is at hand
and that it soon will be time
to cook dinner and roll chapatis.

The phone always showed
while casually exploring
the temperature
or the people in the classroom
talked about how hot 37 degrees feels
and now as I stand in the kitchen making tea
the toast suddenly feels a little too hot
the coconut oil for the post bath toddlers' massage
is already half melted in the bowl
so I realise
It must be summer now.

–46–

Raindrops in a Letter Box

I sent you a rain shower.
Unlike a note,
no one will eavesdrop,
and in its heart,
it carries not a question.

Let it embrace you,
roll itself on your hairy arm,
slide on the bridge of your nose,
and fill your ears,
with the sound of a gift,
pouring over you,
with abundant mercy.

At its core, this rain,
shall wash over the memory,
of the day we parted.
You said, "Nothing is Absolute",

These drops will wash away your doubts.
You said, "Feelings change",
Let the heavens clean your soul.
You said, "I choose to be free",
Oh, Mad One,
Let the water remind you,
That the scent of freedom,
borrows from love,
its very essence,
and all of its existence.

To be loved, and to love back,
if this is not liberation,
What then is?

Pour oh Rain, Pour!
Let him be reminded,
of what life is.

–47–

For Inara

If I write a sonnet for you,
What will it look like?
Will it smell of hybrid tea roses?
Can I contain magic in a verse?
Let me then try to write,
Of your heavenly eyes and,
The beauty of your being,
And the marvel that you are,
The gentleness with which you say 'mama',
And the tenderness with which you hold my hand.
It's not just my heart that smiles,
My entire core resounds,
With the sound of peace,
When I see you!

–48–

What Counts as Everything?

I am making this journey,
from void to void,
traversing through,
endless sutras,
of other worldly realms.

We're still in dialogue,
irrespective of our silences.
Your breath marks,
my beating heart,
my chanting contains,
your unsaid prayers.

Universe after Universe,
we meet in the treasure tower,
conjoined with desire and purpose,
we find the meaning of our lives.
What's there then to be said?
It has all been expressed.

Il y a la tranquillité,
il y a de la beauté,
Il y a la paix,
n'est-ce pas tout?

–49–

When Parvati Married Rahul

Remember that boy,
Who promised you stars?
Poetry, music, art,
Infinite dreams from afar.

Today he spots a grey moustache,
And has learnt to flip a crepe,
But he's still as absent,
As gods from their temples.

Look how this other one stands,
The man in a suit,
Watching over your miseries,
And smiling at your joys.

What if the birds don't chirp,
Or the clouds fade or,
The Amber's turn cold,
This one's right next to you.

There's food on the table,
There's a fan overhead,
No occasion's lonely,
There's fresh linen on the bed.

When the rivers feel alone,
They don't choose to halt,
They flow with sand or leaves,
Or beauty of love for the ocean.

There are streams,
that eternally wind,
through varied paths of continuity,
from your heart to theirs.

–50–

To a Photographer

One said that the colours are ethereal,
When God created the Earth,
Or when the world created itself,
They all forgot about La Manche,
And today it stands – in its arch beauty,
Azure, Cobalt, Cerulean, Lapis!

One said that feeling blue,
Never really meant drear,
The horizon ever so gleams,
And draws in a chimaera,
Of human quest for expanding,
Beyond phenomenon.

One said the man in the picture is her son,
And look how he looks!
He's all the weight of the frame,
And that his only presence,

Gives meaning to this scene,
For the rest exists for his eyes.

One saw the birds and philosophised,
On the flight, the strife and homecomings,
One saw tides approaching & receding,
And questioned the ebb and flow,
What has been and what will be,
And how time itself's stuck in a loop.

When all one by one'd thoroughly analysed,
The Water, The Earth, The Air, The Fire,
Their eyes turned to a silent me,
And questioned as to what I see,
Having heard them post their rigorous scans,
They questioned, "What do you understand?"
I looked at it with supple eyes and sighed,
"I love the hand."

–51–

There are Ways to Burn

There are ways to burn!
To immolate yourself,
In the lustful fire of passion,
Every step is a vapour,
Ending in a flame,
Near the loins of the lover.

To burn long and slow,
In the ever lit ardor of love,
Inspired, warm, combustible,
Melting down walls and bodies,
Emanating light.

To lay kindly in simmering ambers,
In the long gone days of zest,
Hoping and waiting for an occasional night,
Or a tender day of touch,
Mirroring reality.

There are ways to burn,
Ay! I burn for you,
On some days aglow, scorched some,
Doused with your hot eyes, or,
Snug with your cold words,
Acutely, ignited or smouldering,
I do, I burn for you.

–52–

In a Decade's Time

Till a few years back,
I used to come home and change out of the uniform,
Open the diary and see the list of homework.

A glass of milk with bournvita in the evening,
And random conversation about
odd/even roll numbers on the landline.

For many such seasons,
June meant hours and hours of TV,
While March noons meant,
a two-wheeler rush for ṭuition,
Some Saturdays meant,
forgetting to polish white canvas shoes,
Monday recesses would see,
the buckles of the belt fighting to come off.

Assignments, house tests and the days of the annual result,
Those strange and sudden acne and swelling boobs,

Upper lip hair and first time legs' wax,
Street gossip and hand written B'day party invitations,
Crushes, anxieties, career dilemmas.

All of this, was My Life.

Sitting in a different house now,
In casual clothes and Meg Ryan's hair style
I sense a feeling of sloth about folding the blanket.

Or serving fruit to everyone.
Or doctorate deadlines for the thesis submission.

Fretting about pending tasks and unclosed word files,
Staring at a pile of unread books,
The mirror reveals some white hair,
Interspersed with a newly born double chin,
Body, perpetually needing more coffee.

Among the usual doses of medicine,
The necessity of working out,
Planning the June trips with husband,
Crocheting wool bands in winters for the elders,
Weary of toiling to earn money,

I am a different person today
…
but perhaps this is the same life.

–53–

Hooks

How long did it take,
For Newton to realise that,
The apple falling from above,
Is no coincidence.

It took billions of years,
For Earth to find its orbit,
Dinos took millions more to go,
And world web is only just born.

Many times when Mahiwal,
crossed the path of an unknown Sohni,
Or when Antony sat,
Right opposite to Queen Cleo.

How long, O! How long,
Would it have taken them,
To know that like Emily's pair,
They were born of the same salt?

Rome wasn't built in a day, they say,
Nor does Frangipani blossom overnight,
Isn't it then quite unfair of me,
To not peacefully wait for a sign?

In a minute the universe alters,
In another, AI may take its roots,
And yet, wine is best when it ages,
And yet, love's savoured most when awaited.

–54–

A New Reader

Someday you burst through me,
And become the bed where I lay,
I can feel your chest and,
The few tender hair.

The invisible arrest of my soul,
Beneath the air heavy with scents,
I shed a tear,
out of painful joy,
of being in your arms.

Your hands filter the right emotions,
Into the skin of my back,
You fine tune my being.

I float like a fragrant fish,
In the pond of love,
With you.

You don't have to be present,
For your presence,
You are me, I am you,
Can no longer tell,
Where one stops and the other begins.

I love you, I say,
Into imaginary air,
Before the door lock opens,
and steps in,
finding me next to just a pillow,
Another man.

–55–

Birthdays for Broken People

I know where dead people go when they die.
But do you know where go,
The broken ones?

They sit on graves unable to see the grass,
And they travel to temples unable to meet the Gods,
They eat the tasteless moments
Unable to digest that their fears
Have all come to life.

The broken ones…
They create songs in silence
But refuse to write,
Paint their tumbled houses green
But no olives agree to grow.

There are no doves for them,
Nor roses,

They walk on the fragile ropes
That break in an instant
Only for them to land
In a gravity free black hole.

The darkness envelopes them
And their lungs forget to breathe
Rains don't drench them
There's no mud on their feet.

Their nails grow and their eyes carry the bags,
Their hearts, more brittle than the split ends
Of their hair, that carry the memory
Of a past lover,
Ache – quietly.

–56–

An Unasked Question

I don't know what would he say.
That boy who looked outside the window,
As the dusty chalk scribbled and scratched,
No no no,
This solar system's just not done right,
Or do you know that stars have legs?
His mind thought of an Earthly garden,
Where he could sit and not think.

Should he say no,
The winds shall dwindle,
But the clock will move just right,
The cashier will unlock the cash drawer,
Count every little note,
of overmarked, overpriced,
Tiny, accepted bamboozlement,
Meted out to this pink haired punk,
Or that half toothed granny.

Should he say yes,

I should then bring him a multiverse.

Can I send him flowers?

Could petals not fly?

How then for a perfume?

After he's lost all taste for love?

A little verse should then suffice.

Telling him that it's a dance that he doesn't have to dance alone,

That the beach shall have its share of sand slipping under the toes,

But that the squirrels don't always forget where they hid the nuts,

We didn't come this far for nothing,

We came, maybe for words, maybe for pictures, maybe for us!

Us, that dived into the bay,

Only to fly.

To count years with the mind,

Let a fire merge, with another,

For some golden ashes,

That scatter across the land,

Only to contain and cater to,

the life force for,

New Blossoms.

–57–

Treasure Hunt

It was only a dream
replayed in my mind tons of times:
your warmth
your fallen pieces
the sunshine on your lips

…

side by side
you never knew how to say it
the dew on the flowers
or the nectar on my lips

…

between the spaces
just before boarding
you whispered 'aloha' to the wind

…

the stars that shone on us
the sound of your shutters

…

we sought what we found.

–58–

Yeses and Noes

Oh No No, Yes!

There's poetry in a Yes/ in a No.

Did she make it? Yes! (Triumph)

Did you lose? No! (Sigh)

Are we there? Yes! (Excitement)

Are you angry? No! (Relief)

Do you love me? Yes! (Calm)

Did you get hurt? No! (Thankful)

Did you pass? Yes! (Bravo)

Did your phone get erased? No! (Succour)

Is it a holiday today? Yes! (Refreshing)

Has the coffee expired? No! (Well)

Did they arrest the culprit? Yes! (Just)

Is he an addict? No! (Check)

Do I matter to you? Yes! (Value)

Is it too crowded? No! (Respite)

Are you happy? Yes! (Goal)

Any doubts? No! (Confidence)

Is living beautiful? Yes! (Faith)
Is life easy? No (Truth)
Is this a poem? Yes! (Self-assurance)
Does it go to the closet? No! (Release)
Yes needs No, No knows Yes,
Yes?

–59–

Anchors

There's always something to be said of the trees,
that reach out to each other,
or people, who walk back,
to open a window or to,
remind you that they won't leave.
That sometimes,
it's vital for the cocoon to break,
the struggle that chrysalis faces,
or the hardening of a grain of sand,
that a mussel executes,
is the magic contained in the pearls,
or a butterfly's wings.

What isolation gives,
cannot be honoured in public,
And what grows out of the crowd,
will never be at home in solitude.

Do people make a place?
or do places make memories
in themselves?
A book can truly change a mind,
But what is it to a book,
that the reader changed?
The places shall flourish,
the books will line across shelves,
many will come, age and die,
many will bloom, age and wither,
but the trees that reach out,
and the people who come back,
Will Stay.

–60–

Stay

No matter where I am,
Standing out from the crowd,
Or blending in,

No matter what I do,
Right to my own courage,
Or siding with untrue many,

No matter where I turn,
Facing the dawn,
Or hiding in the twilight,

No matter how I save myself,
Sliding under the roller,
Or encountering it head on,

No matter what comes and goes,
In Future or Today,

I am here to stay,

For all the unknown tomorrows,

And uncertainities underway.

–61–

An Eternal Symphony

You didn't have to ask,
My hands sought no permission either,
You touched me not like I was yours,
But like you were mine.
We neither went around the fire,
Nor did anywhere sign,
You had no promises to make,
No rings, no dreams to fake,
You came like cupid,
To his Psyche to touch,
Her soul and her self,
Forever to clutch.

I contained you not like it was you,
But like me to myself unwind,
Into an eternal symphony.

–62–

On Anniversary

Times when your love for me would diminish,
Never arrived through these three years,
For your love has deeply established,
It's strength over all lovers' fears.

The days when you wouldn't be kind,
Never saw the morning sun,
For your generosity forever binds,
All varieties of marital respects into one.

What life had been before you,
And what life has been with you,
Are two ends of eternally separated poles,
For knowing you has changed my all!

Whatever the world May say,
We know it's true,
Beauty lies more in the possessor,
Than the beholder can know.

Your gentleness, your tenderness,
Made a feather bed for my fights,
You touched my life with such finesse,
All darkness submerged into lights.

To love you comes easy,
Like a gently flowing river,
Like a field full of daises,
Waiting for its lovers.

You picked beautiful pieces of my struggles,
And turned them into a marvellous mosaic,
That now stands magically strong amongst the muggles,
Casting its poetry among the prosaic.

In three years your love has given me plenty,
Happiness, delight, confidence and pride,
And the most magnificent of all bounty,
Our lovely little baby bouncing by our side.

Of all that I have done,
Or whatever I am,
The best decision I ever took,
Was to hold your hand.

I thank you for all of this peace,
These showers of blessing, this bliss,
Here's a hug for you dear husband,
And here's this verse, sealed with a kiss!

–63–

Immortal Machine

All his economic life,
Was spent with thrift,
He peddled away his way,
Through rock dead bricks.

His broken seat,
Was the only luxury,
His small pocket,
Could ever contain.

That first day,
When behind him sat,
His newly wedded bride,
Holding his waist with glorious pride.

This world on wheels seemed like,
The greatest gift of life,
That his poorly rich self,
Had ever so begotten.

That bicycle still stands,
Years after he's gone,
On the same rock dead bricks,
Under which somewhere,
Lie buried,
The songs he sang,
The dreams he had,
The love he shared.

And though, he died
His old machine…
It's…still alive!

–64–
You & I

Do we expect,
A cod to know,
Wonders of the stars,
Or vice-versa,
Can a bird remotely grasp,
The depth of waters,
Much beyond its reach?

They will never reach,
The serenity of your being,
This cyclone world,
Would not understand,
The artist in you,
The poet in me,
Let us go then,
You and I,
To lands unknown,
Where prevails the,

Freedom of the mind,

Where we live on a small farm.

You plant veggies,

I water them,

We live a small existence,

Our humble breads on stove,

But Richness of lives,

Let us go then,

You and I.

–65–

Professor Prufrock

Is it not for me to change the world?
To soak seeds overnight,
in deeply filtered water,
and to get them touched by sunshine
till they sprout…

Into their truest selves,
emotionally compartmentalized in shelves,
of complaisant or hysterical nights,
To abide by the dictates of a
blindfolded White woman…

Who regularly comes to lecture halls
and stares out of the window with curious eyes,
Or sits in the staff room sipping black tea
with heavily conditioned hair…
That Herculean logging in and off the wall.

The coos are precious or are they,
more poetic than the Gyre or the Styx?
The long roads with bright lights,
make the dialogue potent,
and slice the agony of monotony.

For they have gone and come back,
before me and shall, after,
Will the Luthers revolt or
would Simone cry?
It is for the fruit to answer.

–66–

Little Things

It was going to be the little things,
Flipping through the pages of a local newspaper,
Reading my name in the op-ed,
Or looking out for the captions,
Under your photographs in print.

Why is my tea still sweet?
Though your cup has the sugar,
I suppose you mixed up the saucers.
The milk's thicker too.

Between the pages of history,
Why do we keep switching places?
The other day you slept on the floor
Some time back I walked out the door.

What's with this toothpaste you like so much?
It's too strong for my gums.
Try my pineapple pudding,
Trust me – it's better than your chocolate.

The landline ringing,
The reminder letter for insurance,
The credit card bill,
Your cousin's birthday party,
Our gazing at the full moon together,
My missing a period.

It was going to be the little things.

–67–

Abohar/ Where I'm From

The subject of this poem,
is a city whose name resembles,
an English word,
you'd rather not want to live in.

In monsoons,
the lanes would flood till knees,
with brown dirty water,
that made for a thrifty pool,
for middle-class children,
who rushed to grab papers for boats,
and floated them across to a neighbour.

The children in school,
were prone to hair lice,
and meanness.
The answers in the final tests,
had to be just the words,

the half-read, average-bred teacher,
insisted on memorising by rote.

Everyone here knew everyone else,
the 'Bintas' and 'Kakas' and 'Paarus'.
The street numbers ran from a simple 1 to 12
and carried gossip in the very air.

My gym instructor started by telling me,
how very short I was,
An uncle in the party expressed worry,
about who would marry my puny being,
My chemistry teacher expressed,
that my poems are unoriginal,
And drawing master hit my palm with a duster,
saying "Tumse Nahin Hoga".

The dreary loo hugged the faces of children,
returning from school in green autos,
The seasonal falsa and shehtoot,
formed our summer delights,
while winters in this townlet saw,
grannies sitting on cots in patios outside,
knitting ponchos for their grandchildren.

Those narrow streets,
Those wide gaps in awareness,
Those interfering eyes,

Those inconsiderate hearts,
Those unpainted walls,
Those broken roads,
Those big disparities,
In those small spaces,
In one corner of the world,
and in a big corner of my mind,
lives this city, which,
despite its shortcomings,
fills my being, on every visit,
with a sense of,
Homecoming.

–68–

Dissolution

Won't thou touch my spine?
Count the tremors you caused.
Won't thou delay a while,
Measure the din you arose.
Onto you, let me evolve,
Into you, let me dissolve.
Through my fingertips let thy bones feel,
The magic of love down till your heel.
Won't you exhale helpless moans,
Stemming from erogenous zones.
Let the rhythm of our forms align,
Consummate, to sing melodies divine.

Nothing could be deeper,
Nothing could be darker,
Than this concentrated dissolution,
And this dissolving concentration,
So let our desires converge,

Gather our whole selves up,
To unite,
And become one colour-

– The colour of Intensity

–69–

Chaap Tilak

All the times we have spoken,

the magic of your voice,

has left on my skin,

right under the surface,

(every word you said)

a trace.

I touch my arm,

or my toes,

to revisit,

one part or another,

of a conversation,

about comics books,

or what magic is,

or just about anything.

Going back and forth in time,
I revise a memory,
or revive a feeling,
tips of my fingers,
unfolding one of your expressions,
or your ever so gentle laughter,
that causes my heart to smile.

I touch my body,
little by little,
unfurling the poetry,
etched by your words,
and read them, line by line,
through the sensations,
that my nerves carry,
and thereafter,
the veins pulsate with.

You have turned me,
into a long verse,
that waits to be sung,
through the instrument,
of your being,
or,
into a painting,
of artistic strokes,
that derives its colours,
from the sound of your voice.

–70–

Cloudy Day

The Sun felt bored to be so free to shine,

Upon its lover earth,

So some restrictions Nature did provide,

In way of its light, to liberally disperse.

Water loved the sky very much,

At last, it confessed and avowed,

Volunteered in draping ether,

By transforming into clouds.

Caressing and cuddling heaven's bosom,

It beatified his valentine,

And happier was the sun,

To touch his paramour in new designs.

Through patterns in art attaining their bourn,

Two eternal unities thus were born,

Emerging out of Love,

To shade & sketch below & above.

–71–

Emperor of Maxims

Nietzsche came into my dream,
and wrote some poetry,
on the green board,
in a grey classroom.
…something about the evil,
and how the good shall never suffice.

I sat like an ardent learner,
quite assured that,
I understood,
What FN Sir was trying to say,
while others around me felt offended.
How can kindness stem from contempt?
How can being freer mean being lonelier?
How can old friends become ghosts of our own past?

What pleases eagerly,
is forgotten easily.

What offends crudely,
instructs deeply.
There are as many truths,
as there are points of view.

Isn't wrong just another side of right?
Isn't right much likely to go wrong?
Who are, then, we to forgive?
Man often deifies what he defies,
and more often than not,
defies what he deifies.

"Reality is a flux", he wrote,
"Isn't everything then, just,
a changing face of change?",
I thought, just as the sun broke
in, from the slit in the curtain,
And woke me up,
to a deeply structured
social reality;
that would require
a hundred other Nietzsche
and many such dreams,
to alter its fixated fizzog.

–72–

Theseus in Love

Where is the life I dreamt of?
Those delicate touches,
And endless dreaminess!
That secret excursion and
You, holding me gently…

There's a life in my buried dream,
That reminds me it's alive.
In the middle of the night,
I wake up to greet it,
Adore it, live it, pen it,
For once the reality shuts the door,
My garden's hijacked with truth.

Whose truth? You may ask,
The one that the world thinks is or,
The one that you affirm to me silently?
Both faces are mine, both are not untrue.

But the purity of these dreams,

The strength of my recollection,

And the earnestness in my imagination,

Are all the core of my being.

I love you like the lonely stars in the sky love darkness,

I love you like an empty heart craves for existence,

I love you like a transplanted tree which has never forgotten its real home,

I love you beyond the reach of this world's biggest reality and, farther than beyond the depth of feelings I've ever known.

I love you. Stay with me.

–73–

To Living Alone

Find me a lover then,
in the corners of my own mind, filled with
self-love and independence and a
hundred million blogs about 'abundance within'.
Find me then, a touch of my own hand,
at the nape of my neck, and a
candle light partner,
in the form of my unpublished manuscript.
Let my mirror then recite to me
ditties of love in tune with a stringed Uke.
Tell my other half
to share the other half of a peach
and let it as well,
take fancy pictures of me
as I bake a pie for two,
to savour it by myself or as I swim
with poise, to get the desired curves
for my Saturday night hand-holding

"soirée romantique solo!"
worthy of raising a toast to my
postmodern, healthy and so called
psychologically balanced existence.

–74–

Unhitched

In the end,
We only live with ourselves.
Nothing belongs to us,
and we belong to no one.

A little less sugar,
or some extra bit of milk,
And there goes
our perfect cup of tea,
stumbling into compromises.

All of our broken pieces,
hang on to certain talismans,
our little fetishes,
making junkets through worlds,
at the expense of our future dreams.

It is true that pain blinds ethics,
and love, unless causes it,
eases out the pain.
Wasn't Batalvi right all along?
It's assuredly being born,
that kills us, but death
gratuitously takes the blame,
for the lack of our sagacity.

–75–

Peut être/ A Possibility

My personal apocalypse,
Looked as lovely as a
Lone dandelion growing
Beside a drying lake.

When sun falls on his neck,
He thinks of my gaze
And quietly blinks his eyes,
Breathing out,
Suspiring,
A possibility.

Those unknown fears,
Kept him from acting,
On his desires.
His insecurities,
Withhold the words,
That his soul yearns,
To release.

Intention,
Is the real distance,
Between two people.
And Love,
Is the only reason,
For Happiness in life to become,
Worth fighting for.

On quiet evenings,
The fume of his tea,
Or a sudden downpour,
Will hold his hand,
And walk him down,
Our memory lane,
Where maybe on a silent bench,
He would find me sitting,
With a vacant seat next to me.

–76–

Towards Kosen-rufu

All happiness,
at its heart attracts pain.
One day after another,
uncertainty knocks at the door
with a box of doughnuts, sometimes,
sometimes, a postcard with a sad news.
No wonder we're all broken,
terrified of being lonely,
searching corners here and there for love,
in one particular form alone.

Water, water, everywhere,
and not a drop's the same.
How varied they are:
drops in a pond,
waves in a sea,
falling snowflakes,
tides in an ocean,

raindrops from the sky,
icecaps and glaciers,
hot springs.

And yet,
sunset after sunset,
our desires rise, gladly bringing in
misery.
The little flowers are content,
this ant, that moth, they're the
true Bodhisattvas of the Earth.
Sunrise after sunrise, they
set their days, drop by drop,
in a sheer attempt at being alive;
in loving and being loved,
(sans pressure on their lips)
just as they both come.

–77–

To Preyaan

On Sundays,
my scion wakes up earlier,
than any other working-for-school
day of the week.

He knows not the expression,
but understands the excitement of,
'Dolce far niente'
and brings out his stack of hot wheels,
lines them up outside my door,
and honks the horn with a,
guttural 'brrrrr', followed by beep, beep.

I emerge,
with usual mildly swollen,
hypothyroid fingers,
and break his hypothetical journey
into an automotive multiverse,

with a cup of cardamom milk,
and a pair of crocs with a strict disapproval of his bare feet.

Where are our real Sundays?
Free of hours and
devoid of motherly instructions?
As I question myself,
my heart fills with self deprecation,
then, as I take off my slippers,
to jump into imaginary puddles,
I convince myself,
that's it's true that moon rises to greet him,
that his plastic thermometer is quite accurate,
that his paper cookies will get baked in the refrigerator,
that it is his turn again after his turn on the carrom board,
and that in his multiverse of luxury cars,
his three year and 8 month old self
can drive me safely to Gotham city.

–78–

Ellipsis

Ellipsis ~
Is the silence
Between two lover
Who mutually agreed
On quietude.

…

Is the distance between
The last words
That the father wanted to say
To the son who departed
A little too early.

…

Is the answer
To all the questions
That intellectuals ask
And the universe
Cannot respond to.

...
Is the war cry
That no one heard
Or the crushed buttercup
That no one noticed, was
Painted on the road

...
Is our selves
Between the smiles
we truly don't mean
And the tears
We force ourselves to cry.

Short Poems

1.

This is a Happy Poem.
No one is dying here
No Truths are told.
The father is always a hero,
and the lover never hurts.

2.

Take me beyond this land,
Take me towards the riverside,
Close to that field where he promised to meet,
That boy, who quoted Rumi to me.

3.

Not all obstructions
Barr Freedom,
Not all windows,
Grant It.

4.

A Brave woman dares
Her passion ensnares
Her fears of failure!

A Brave woman deems
The truth in her dreams
To be the reality unseen!

5.

An amalgam of restless thoughts
Minute by minute, wrought
Ideas – so diverse, so many
Eulogies, elegies – I'm a bard gone uncanny.

6.

I tell myself
It even blooms on a tombstone,
"You still breathe, you can't stink."

7.

Drowned in Dust, Drawn as a demon,
Darkness that no words could hold,
She was but a passionate woman,
And that became her only fault.

8.

I wake up from soft sleep
Many-a-hair gather on my cheek
You, who lie next to me,
Bring yourself closer to see,
With gentle fingers you brush them aside.
My half opened eyes onto your face glides,
With closed eyes I fall back on thine,
To touch your tender lips with mine.

9.

I, Too,
Overflow,
With a sense of rapture,
In myriad shades
Of pleasure and meek fury,
Stimulated to rewrite,
My history into eternity.

10.

Into such grubbiness my passion descends,
Into such mediocrity it suspends,
That I seek the help of 'words'
And gestures outwards,
And all this while, You,
Knowing the depth of things,
Knowing how words shall never suffice,
Let 'love' grow unspoken and inwards.

11.

The roaring Tiger of Religion,
On the bloody wheel stands,
Its fiercely ruddy eye & conniving whiskers,
The horde of hurdles – disband,
On goes the world in swift motions,
None but the "Poets" withstand.

12.

Ponds of Water,
In the faulty Pits
That After-rain
Could not drain…

…Are pools of pleasure
To the scarred limbs
That Labour pain
Could not contain.

13.

Love is an essence, which binds,
The redness of your heart with mine.
Love is a flower that finds,
Its blossoming exuberance in summer sunshine.
Delicately woven into colourful purity,
Our love finds its innocent maturity.

14.

Under the dim lights,
You were here tonight,
Just as real as my imagination,
You spoke what I desired,
You looked the way I pictured,
You acted like I wanted,
My hard stoned heart,
For a moment,
Forgot our long series of 'nothings',
Under this one 'something'…

15.

Behind the shadow of my dreams,
And some childish castles I built,
Stands reality like a small weed.
Ever growing, ever thriving,
Slowing heading towards the fort.
I guard the doors, I wo-man them,
One of us will shut out the other,
Depending on whether I accept,
Or assert.

16.

He was the most colourless boy
To have walked under sepia toned trees
Coarse, uneven and fragmented,
He was all that damp Earth can be.

But I,
I loved him.

In his lap I grew,
With sprouting victory
And his hidden beauty of depth,
Coloured every inch of me.

17.
She drank the hydrous desire,
From that eternal spring,
The flow of water acquired,
Her every-imagined-thing,
She hung through those outpourings,
Till their echo in her core ringed.

Aqua's enchanted song,
Played those unheard chords,
Folded between her palms,
The music of her destiny,
Raging within her veins,
Ready to burst,
an intrinsic torrent.

18.

Syllables uttered
Through my tongue
Go out and touch him
On his eardrum
Much beyond inside
Its echo rings.

He never has to say a thing,
In terms or deeds,
He is. He just is.

19.

I felt like making something for you,
and found no icing sugar,
plucking the flowers will be brutal,
and harp, I know not how to play,
Drawing was never my talent,
and embroidery was nowise my art.

So what do I get you?

I am getting you my core's breath,
the music of my smiling lips,
the unending yearning to smell your hand,
and the taste of bliss under closed eyelids,
the fond touch of dew on a folded bud,
and these few words on a screen.

20.

They do cardio with your dreams,

Squats with your originality,

And crunches with your hopes.

It ain't done yet!

Your verse pressed down the bench,

And your pain pushed up the rod,

Your feeling trod upon,

And pressure planked on,

With such social methods,

Emerges,

Your beautiful disfigurement.

21.

There, in the little corner,

Where I hid all unfulfilled dreams,

There, in that corner, I found

My source of light.

22.

She was a sunflower,

Who decided to rename herself.

Why should the sun define her life?

Why must she turn at his bidding?

Must she bend?

Must she rise?

She must rise!
Grab freedom that's hers,
Undo her genetic code,
Choose her own colour,
Decide on her form,
Triumph her thoughts,

And BLOSSOM!

23.

Perhaps the hollowness inside
was the premonition
of having you so near
and then losing you forever.
And now that hollowness
stares at itself in the mirror
and knows that it's not an imitation.

24.

Life lay in her brown hands like cream pearls,
Glossy, Elegant and Pure,
She just had to keep the fingers bent inwards,
To protect its Beauty from,
Eyes of the green-eyed world,
And the declension inflicted by Time.

25.

There comes that time,

When wheels of life *retire,*

Buried under the soil,

Or burned over a *pyre*

To dust turn the eyes,

To ashes – the inner *fire,*

One more round completes the soul,

Up or down that *gyre,*

When nothing's left to see,

To feel or to *inspire,*

It's only 'words' that'll save us,

From the entire *quagmire.*

26.

In every love relationship

the traces of the first one

break in. The takeaways

and the heartache

the lessons,

like the dried up outline

of water on muram floor,

it exists, refining,

and defining,

coeval matters of the heart.

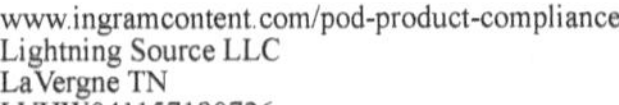